"It was on Easter Monday, April 9, 1917,
and not on any other date,
that Canada became a nation."

— D. J. Goodspeed, *The Road Past Vimy*

AT VIMY RIDGE

Canada's Greatest World War I Victory

Hugh Brewster

SCHOLASTIC CANADA LTD.

April 9, 1917 – Before dawn on that Easter morning, big flakes of snow began falling over Vimy Ridge. For the Canadian soldiers huddled in darkness below the ridge, the snow was a reminder of home. Many of them had just written letters to those they loved back in Canada. "This may be a note of farewell," wrote one, "for we attack tomorrow morning." All of them knew that the ridge that loomed ahead of them was a fearsome enemy stronghold. They knew that the French and the British had tried to take it and failed. But they had planned and rehearsed this attack for months. And for the first time, the four Canadian divisions would be fighting together, 100,000 strong. Just as the sky began to lighten, the whole world seemed to shudder as 983 enormous guns fired as one. This was the moment for the Canadians to advance.

THE MARKETS.
Canadian, New York, and London closed.
Winnipeg October wheat closed 2⅝c higher
at 98½c.

The Globe.

THE WEATHER.
Probabilities :—Fair and warmer; thunder-showers at night.
The sun rises at 5.10 a.m. and sets at 7.37 p.m.
Next British mail, via the Empress of Britain, from Quebec, closes to-day at 6 p.m.

VOLUME LXXI.   TORONTO, WEDNESDAY, AUGUST 5, 1914—SIXTEEN PAGES.   NUMBER 20,138.

GREAT BRITAIN AND GERMANY ARE NOW AT WAR

LONDON, Aug. 4.—The British Foreign Office has issued the following statement :—"Owing to the summary rejection by the German Government of the request made by his Britannic Majesty's Government that the neutrality of Belgium should be respected, his Majesty's Ambassador at Berlin has received his passports, and his Majesty's Government has declared to the German Government that a state of war exists between Great Britain and Germany from 11 o'clock p.m., August 4."

THE BULWARK OF BRITAIN'S EMPIRE GOES FORTH AGAIN TO BATTLE

King George Says the Navy Will Revive Its Glories in Action

A Dramatic Scene as the King and the Statesmen of Britain Waited the Striking of the ... ich Meant War—Stirring Message ... the First Sign That Hos-... G. Wells Tells How

Billions Voted

(Canadian Press Despatch.)
London, Aug. 4.—The House of Commons voted $525,000,000 for emergency purposes, and passed several bills in five minutes without a dissentient voice to-day.

Berlin, Aug. 4.—A bill was introduced into the German Imperial Parliament to-day providing for the appropriation of $1,250,000,000 to meet the expenses of the war. It was passed.

MR. ASQUITH'S STORY OF THE ULTIMATUM

Germany's Amazing View of Neutrality Agreement

Britain Could Not Accept It in Any Way as Satisfactory, Said the Premier, and Therefore Sent an Ultimatum to Germany.

(Canadian Press Despatch.)
London, Aug. 4.—Premier Asquith in the House of Commons to-day confirmed the sending to Germany of a request that she should give the same assurance of the neutrality of Belgium as Fr... her reply...

WAR SUMMARY

IT IS WAR. Diplomacy has said the last word, and the diplomats have separated wrangling—even after their taxis had been ordered—as to who was really to blame. The sword must now settle the controversy. It will be a terrific struggle waged all over the world. Into the vortex have already been drawn Germany and Austria on the one hand, and Servia, Russia, France, Belgium and Great Britain on the other. Italy and Turkey may yet join Germany and Austria, and Holland will probably take a part in the desire to secure an easy the Belgians and their allies in seeking to safeguard the independence of the Low Countries against German aggression.

* * * * *

BRITAIN'S PARTICIPATION became inevit-when Germany insisted upon marching ... in the desire to secure an easy ... The fact that Germany

PARLIAMENT CALLED FOR AUGUST 18TH

Army Division of 23,000 to be Mobilized

PROTECTING VITAL POINTS

Armed Forces Guarding Ports and Cable and Wireless Stations—Will Protect Canals and Other Means of Transportation and Communication

The Canadian Parliament is summoned to meet on Tuesday, August 18, to vote funds for Imperial defence and to decide on the disposal of the Canadian forces. The order ... bilization of ...

"The country went mad!" is how one veteran described the mood when war was declared (left). Patriotic rallies (opposite) stressed Canada's links to the British Empire. Even posters in Quebec (opposite, centre), featured Britain's flag and urged French-Canadians to help "crush the tyranny" of German Kaiser Wilhelm II (below). Soon parades of recruits (opposite, right, top) were seen on city streets.

**"Everyone just jumped up and wanted to go to war. . . .
You know, banners waving and bands playing! It was just like a fever."**

— Jack Burton, Fredericton

WAR FEVER August 4, 1914

Almost three years before Vimy, the news that war had been declared was greeted with wild enthusiasm all across Canada. In Montreal, surging crowds sang "God Save the King," "La Marseillaise" and "O Canada" in both languages. A brass band marched along King Street in Toronto, leading a singing, flag-waving parade. In Winnipeg, hundreds of young men marched to the militia barracks and fought for the chance to enlist.

Canada hadn't declared war, of course; Great Britain had. But that meant that Canada, as a dominion of the British Empire, was at war as well. Most Canadians, in the words of one Toronto newspaper, were "carried away with patriotic enthusiasm at the thought that Britain . . . had decided to give the bully of Europe a trouncing." That bully was Germany, led by its emperor with the bristling moustache, Kaiser Wilhelm II. For years

Germany had been building battleships at an alarming rate, challenging the British navy, which (as everyone knew) "ruled the waves."

Many of the men who rushed off to volunteer that August were afraid that they might miss out on the action. The newspapers said the war could be over by Christmas! For some of them, the army offered an escape from the tedium of farm or factory work, for the pretty decent pay of $1.10 per day. That was along with food, a uniform — and maybe some adventure, as well.

Recruiting young Canadians was a duty that Sam Hughes, the country's minister of militia and defence, tackled with great relish. Sam Hughes believed that Canadian soldiers could teach the British a thing or two about fighting. The day after war was declared, he announced that Canada would send 25,000 officers and enlisted men to fight for the Empire. In 1914 Canada had an army that was about one-tenth that size — although many men volunteered in local militias. Hughes called on every militia unit across Canada to send

" We are Sam Hughes' Army,
Thirty thousand men are we;
We cannot fight, we cannot march,
What bloody good are we."

— a song sung by the Canadian recruits

Sam Hughes' Army

To the governor general he was "a conceited lunatic." Even his boss, Prime Minister Robert Borden, thought Sam Hughes might not be entirely sane. The eccentric Minister of Militia was shrewd enough to make sure that contracts for army supplies went to companies run by his political friends. The result was boots that fell apart when it rained, coats that soaked up water, and horses so old and skinny they had to be destroyed. He championed the Canadian-made Ross rifle, which the soldiers hated as it jammed easily. Both Hughes and his rifle were replaced before the battle of Vimy Ridge.

(Above) At Valcartier, Sam Hughes loved to gallop about on horseback and preside over big parades of marching men — for the cameras. (Left) Hughes was very proud of this shovel, which he had patented. It had an eye-hole so it could be used as a face shield as well as for digging. The shovel proved to be useless; 25,000 of them were scrapped.

volunteers to train at Valcartier, Quebec.

But there was no army camp at Valcartier, only acres of bush. Construction began quickly, but when trainloads of recruits began arriving there in late August, the camp was a shambles. Men were crammed into tents and there were hardly any uniforms for them — far less, rifles and equipment. In the chaos at Valcartier, there was little time for proper training. As one officer wrote in a letter home, "We are in no shape to go into action." By

(Left, top) Men lie in the sun next to some of Valcartier's 8,000 horses. Little real training took place at Valcartier, though some soldiers practised shooting with the Ross rifle. (Left, bottom) Two recruits pose with their bayoneted Ross rifles. By the end of October, the men of the Canadian First Contingent were drilling on Salisbury Plain in England (opposite). Marches and bayonet practice (inset) took place within sight of the ancient monument of Stonehenge.

late September, however, Sam Hughes announced that the 30,617 men of the Canadian Expeditionary Force were ready to sail from Quebec City. "Soldiers," Hughes declared in his farewell message to them, "the world regards you as a marvel." To the men jammed on the ships amid a muddle of horses and equipment, this was a joke.

Once they arrived in England, the Canadian recruits were sent to a training camp on Salisbury Plain. And the British army officers there did not regard them as "a marvel." In fact, they found them to be an undisciplined, untrained rabble. The Canadians, in turn, did not care for the snooty, spit-and-polish attitude of the British. "We came here to fight," they said, "not to salute."

Record rainfall soon turned the English army camp into a mudhole. The miserable conditions meant more delays in training. Nonetheless, by February of 1915, the War Office declared that the first Canadian soldiers were ready to be sent to fight in France. The boys who had rushed to enlist in towns from Victoria to Halifax were about to discover what war was really like.

Canadian Recruits undergo training at Salisbury.

IN THE TRENCHES

By early March of 1915, the 1st Canadian Division was in the trenches near Armentières. Between them and the enemy lines lay only 30 metres of "no man's land" strewn with barbed wire and pockmarked with holes blasted by German guns. Soldiers quickly learned to keep their heads down, as enemy snipers or machine guns could pick off the unwary. Behind the front-line trenches were support trenches through which water, ammunition and food were carried forward. Nobody starved on the diet of corned beef and bread or biscuits

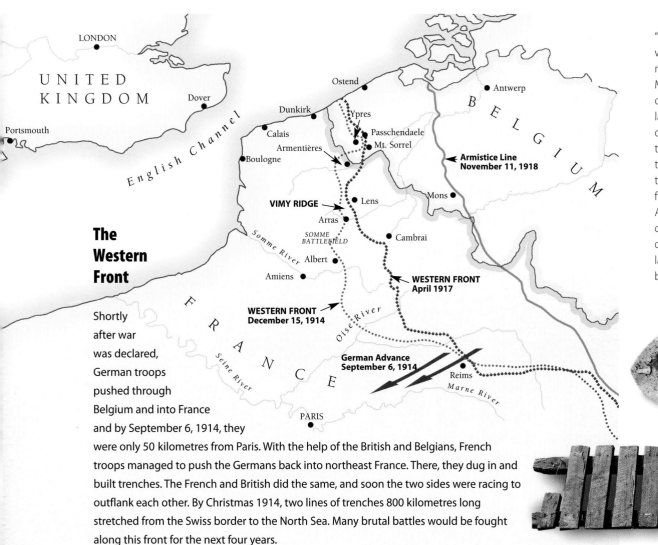

The Western Front

Shortly after war was declared, German troops pushed through Belgium and into France and by September 6, 1914, they were only 50 kilometres from Paris. With the help of the British and Belgians, French troops managed to push the Germans back into northeast France. There, they dug in and built trenches. The French and British did the same, and soon the two sides were racing to outflank each other. By Christmas 1914, two lines of trenches 800 kilometres long stretched from the Swiss border to the North Sea. Many brutal battles would be fought along this front for the next four years.

"Your shovel is your best friend," soldiers were told. (Right) In his mud-caked kilt a member of the Royal Highlanders from Montreal digs out a trench. He stands on one of the wooden duckboards that were laid underfoot. (Below) This shovel and duckboard were recently unearthed on the Western Front. Steel helmets (opposite, top right) were issued to British soldiers in the spring of 1916 to help prevent deaths from head wounds. (Opposite, far right) A smiling soldier lies in the hole he has dug in a trench wall. This will be his home during his time in this trench. Officers had larger dugouts that often had room for a bed and a desk.

with tea and jam, but it left the soldiers feeling permanently hungry. In the first weeks, 100 men were killed or wounded, but this was considered "normal" for the Western Front. In early April, however, the 1st Canadian Division learned they were moving north to a town called Ypres, in Flanders, a part of Belgium. Known as "Wipers" to the soldiers, Ypres had a fearsome reputation as the scene of fierce and bloody fighting.

"Now they speak of trenches . . . trenches is too romantic a name. . . . These were ditches. As time went by we had no garbage [or] sewage disposal. . . . The smell was a sour, strange odour. . . . Wherever you went the whole place was squealing and squeaking with these huge, monstrous rats. . . . And in that setting men lived . . . year after year. . . ."

— Lieutenant Gregory Clark

503 - Attaque aux gaz - Somme -

GAS!

On the evening of April 22, 1915, Canadian soldiers in the trenches near Ypres were shocked to see gasping, retching French soldiers running towards them. "They literally were coughing their lungs out," Major Andrew McNaughton recalled. Poisonous chlorine gas had been released by the Germans. Two days later, greenish-yellow clouds of the deadly vapour seeped towards the Canadian front lines. For protection, the men were told to urinate on their handkerchiefs and to hold them over their noses. This did little good but they kept on fighting — even when their Ross rifles clogged up from mud and rapid firing. Amazingly, the Canadians held their positions until reinforcements came. At the end of the battle, Ypres remained in Allied hands. But the casualties from what became known as the Second Battle of Ypres were appalling — over 6,700 men were killed. The Canadians had proved themselves in battle, but at a terrible cost.

Clouds of approaching gas (left) were a terrifying sight. This aerial photograph of a Somme battlefield shows the wind blowing the gas westward. The first gas hoods (right and opposite left) were hard to see through and had a chemical treatment that irritated the face. Later gas masks, such as the one shown in this painting (above, left) by Frederick Varley, were more effective. (Opposite, upper left) Burns and blisters from mustard gas would scar this soldier for life.

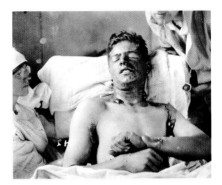

"A man dies by gas in horrible torment. He turns perfectly black . . . he lingers five or six minutes and then — goes West."

— Private Harold Peat, 3rd Battalion

"Their brass buttons were green."

"There were about two hundred to three hundred men lying in that ditch. Some were clawing at their throats. Their brass buttons were green. Their bodies were swelled. Some of them were still alive . . . we thought they were Germans. One inquisitive fellow turned a dead man over. He saw a brass clip bearing the name CANADA on the corpse's shoulder and exclaimed, 'These are Canadians!' Some of us said, 'For the love of Mike! We never knew that!' Some of the Canadians were still writhing on the ground, their tongues hanging out."

— British private David Shand, describing the gas attack near Ypres

"...tens of thousands of our men are lying low, never to rise again. ...As far as my e

kes me, I can see rows of dead. . . . Have lost my old pals today."

— from the diary of English soldier Robert Cude on July 1, 1916

STALEMATE AND SLAUGHTER

Canadians at home were shocked to read the long death lists after the Second Battle of Ypres. And poison gas showed just how cruel modern warfare could be. By the summer of 1915, there were 150,000 men in the Canadian Corps and Prime Minister Robert Borden pledged that it would grow to 500,000 in 1916. But volunteers were no longer storming the recruiting centres. And 1916 would prove to be an even more bloodstained year. In early June, over 8,000 Canadians died in the battle for a single hill called Mont Sorrel. On the first day of July, the battle of the Somme began with one of the worst bloodbaths in history. Near a village called Beaumont-Hamel, 780 Newfoundlanders advanced on enemy lines; only 110 survived unscathed. By the end of that terrible day, 57,470 British Empire soldiers lay dead or wounded. And by the time the Somme offensive ended in November, it had cost Canada 24,029 casualties. Allied losses numbered over 620,000. German deaths put the toll at over one million. And virtually nothing had been gained by either side.

(Opposite) Battle-weary Canadians trudge back through the mud. Their less fortunate comrades lay in shallow battlefield graves like the one shown above. By mid-1916, most Canadians went into battle carrying Lee-Enfield rifles, which fired a 303-cartridge bullet (inset, below) shown here at actual size. (Below, left) A bandaged soldier seems pleased to be one of the walking wounded, while a more serious casualty (below, middle) is loaded into an ambulance wagon. (Below, right) A nurse supervises a patient being loaded onto a train that will take him to hospital. During the war, 2,504 Canadian nurses served overseas and 46 died in the line of duty.

ON TO VIMY

After the slaughter at the Somme, the Allies badly needed to make a breakthrough. But to do so they had to knock out the German bastion of Vimy Ridge. This 15-kilometre-long escarpment north of the French city of Arras commanded a view of the surrounding area that made a surprise attack unlikely. Guns of every kind bristled all along the slope and beneath its muddy surface lay tunnels and caverns carved out of the soft, chalk stone. The Germans considered the ridge to be impregnable. Over 160,000 French and British soldiers had died in attacks on Vimy Ridge since October of 1914. Now the task of capturing it fell to the Canadians. The troops once thought to be untrained, rowdy colonials, were now regarded as one of the most effective fighting forces on the Allied side.

When the Canadians arrived at Vimy in December of 1916, the Germans hoisted a sign saying "Welcome Canadians." On Christmas Day, the men of the Princess Patricia's Light Infantry arranged a truce with some Germans and exchanged rum toasts. But soon both sides returned to their trenches and by evening the gunfire had resumed. And a cold, bitter winter lay ahead of them.

> **"You might be able to get to the top of Vimy Ridge but I'll tell you this: you'll be able to take all the Canadians back in a rowboat that get there."**
>
> — a German officer, captured before the battle of Vimy Ridge

(Above) Canadians set up camp behind the trenches at Vimy. The graves of French soldiers lie in the foreground. (Left) A modern re-enactor poses in full battle gear, from his "tin hat" down to his cloth leggings, called puttees. He holds a Lee-Enfield rifle with bayonet.

ECURIE

to Arras

ROCLINCOURT

17TH COR (BRITISH

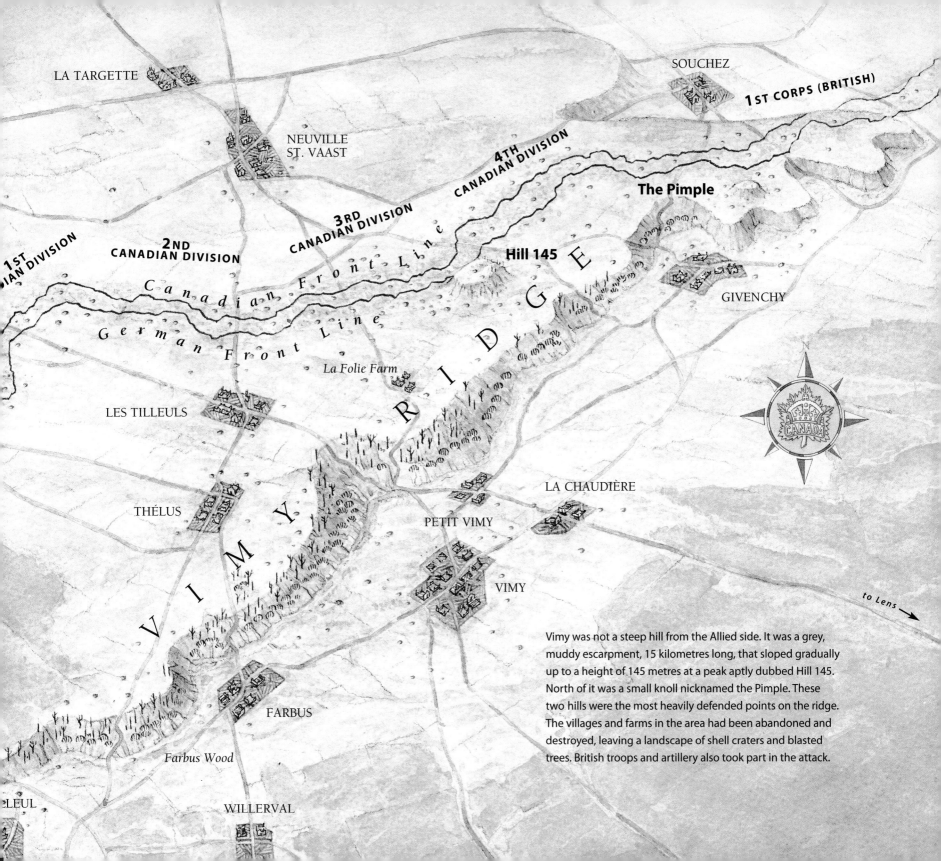

LA TARGETTE

SOUCHEZ

1ST CORPS (BRITISH)

NEUVILLE
ST. VAAST

4TH
CANADIAN DIVISION

The Pimple

3RD
CANADIAN DIVISION

Hill 145

2ND
CANADIAN DIVISION

Canadian Front Line

1ST
IAN DIVISION

C a n a d i a n   F r o n t   L i n e

G e r m a n   F r o n t   L i n e

GIVENCHY

La Folie Farm

R I D G E

LES TILLEULS

V I M Y

LA CHAUDIÈRE

THÉLUS

PETIT VIMY

VIMY

to Lens →

Vimy was not a steep hill from the Allied side. It was a grey,
muddy escarpment, 15 kilometres long, that sloped gradually
up to a height of 145 metres at a peak aptly dubbed Hill 145.
North of it was a small knoll nicknamed the Pimple. These
two hills were the most heavily defended points on the ridge.
The villages and farms in the area had been abandoned and
destroyed, leaving a landscape of shell craters and blasted
trees. British troops and artillery also took part in the attack.

FARBUS

Farbus Wood

LEUL

WILLERVAL

NEGLECTING NOTHING

The Canadians at Vimy liked their commanding officer, General Julian Byng. Unlike many other British officers, he wasn't stuffy or stand-offish. He didn't care about shiny buttons or smart salutes — but he did care about his men. And he wasn't about to see any of them sacrificed because of poor planning. So Byng sent his most trusted Canadian general, Arthur Currie, to learn all he could from the disastrous battles of 1916. Currie was the perfect man for the job. He had an amazing head for detail and was supremely organized — even keeping a "Things to Remember" list. One motto on his list was, "A thorough preparation must lead to success. Neglect nothing."

"We placed absolute trust in our men, and took them entirely into our confidence. We were confident that no one would desert and divulge information. And no one did." — Captain D.C. MacIntyre

(Above, left) Behind the lines, Canadian soldiers study maps similar to the one shown at right. (Above, right) General Arthur Currie (second from left) stands with other senior officers and visiting politicians, as they watch troops in training for battle.

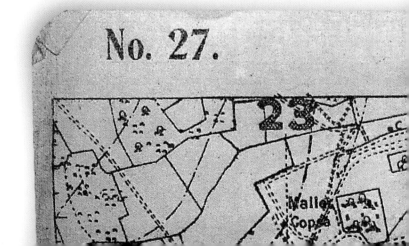

No. 27.

One of Arthur Currie's first recommendations after his fact-finding trip was a simple one: give the men maps. But it was a new idea for the British Army, where maps had always been reserved for officers. So 40,000 maps were created so that each man could mark out where he would advance on the ridge. And each soldier would learn all the details of the attack plan — except for the date. This meant the men were being trusted — rather than being told to follow orders blindly. The boost this gave to morale was huge. Over the next few months, every detail of the attack would be carefully planned and practised — making Vimy the most rehearsed battle in history.

BYNG AND CURRIE Julian Byng, 54, (above, left) was a well-educated English aristocrat. Arthur Currie, 45, (above, right) was an Ontario farmboy with only a high-school education. Byng was an experienced professional soldier; Currie had learned military strategy from books as a weekend warrior in a Victoria, B.C., militia. Byng was lean with a clipped, military moustache; Currie had a pear-shaped build and ample jowls — and, unlike Byng, he was never popular with the men. Yet Arthur Currie became perhaps the greatest general Canada has ever produced.

CANADA

MESSAGE MAP.　　German Trenches

"The air was dank and close."

"They lowered us down . . . to a chalk tunnel. It was cold outside but when we got down there all sound stilled and it was warm. . . . We worked in turns and fast . . . one man cut it with a knife . . . and passed back large chunks to his helper. The chalk was handed back until it reached a small trolley drawn on tracks which took it to the hoist. . . . The air was dank and close and we sweated a great deal. The man in charge forbade anyone speaking. At any moment the removal of a newly-cut chunk might reveal a German dugout filled with men!"

— Will R. Bird,
42nd Infantry Battalion

WAR UNDERGROUND

The front at Vimy was a maze of trenches with names like Stargate Street, Spadina Avenue and Tottenham Road. Beneath them was a honeycomb of caves — some large enough to hold hundreds of men — and tunnels, which were called subways. The Grange Subway, one of the largest, had a main passageway 685 metres long. Off it were side tunnels and underground rooms housing ammunition stores, officers' quarters, a chapel, offices and a huge water tank. Byng and his planners soon realized that the subways could be used in the attack as well. Digging began on twelve subways that would lead right up to — and even past — the attack line. At Zero Hour, the mouths of the subways would be blasted open and the men inside would charge out into the heart of the battlefield.

(Above, left) Two men lift chalk from a tunnel while an officer listens on a geophone, in case Germans are digging nearby. (Opposite, right) A trolley on rails can still be seen in the Grange Subway at Vimy today. Soldiers scratched graffiti in the soft chalk walls of the tunnel, and one carving of a maple leaf (right) has been preserved. (Opposite, left, bottom) The Grange Subway had many underground rooms and was the largest of the twelve tunnels (opposite, left).

GIVENCHY-EN-GOHELLE

LA CHAUDIÈRE

VIMY RIDGE

GERMAN LINE

CANADIAN LINE

Hill 145

PETIT VIMY

VIMY

La Folie Farm •

GRANGE subway

NEUVILLE ST. VAAST

LES TILLEULS

THÉLUS

0   1   2   3km

Part of the GRANGE subway

To Neuville St. Vaast

To the front lines

Exit

Exit

To the rear lines

Munitions store or infirmary

Officers' mess

To the rear lines

Conference hall

Kitchen

Office for Officer of the day

Waiting room

Chapel or storage room

Office for Commanding Officer (CO)

CO's bedroom

Underground lake (drinking water)

"We had blackened faces. . . . We caught those Germans down in their dugout . . . and we brought away twelve quivering prisoners. We had no losses at all . . . it was amazing." — Victor Odlum describing his first trench raid

TRENCH RAIDS

Canadians were good at trench raids. In fact, they'd invented them. And in the four months before the Vimy attack, fifty-five raids were made on German positions. Some raids were quick and needed only a handful of men — others involved hundreds of soldiers and weeks of planning. Julian Byng thought trench raids were good for morale; Arthur Currie thought they were useful only for gathering information. And he thought that big raids put too many lives at risk.

The biggest trench raid of all would prove that Currie was right. Its mission was to damage German defences high on the ridge. It was launched on the morning of March 1, 1917, with the release of clouds of poison gas. But the Germans knew the

Master of the Trench Raid Victor Odlum (right) is given credit for perfecting the trench raid, a surprise attack on the enemy lines at night. Odlum was in command of the 7th (British Columbia) Battalion in November of 1915. His men were bored and cold and someone suggested a raid on the enemy trenches to relieve the monotony. Odlum planned the raid carefully for ten days before attacking. The results were successful and the Canadians became known for their skill at trench raids. The French soon wanted Odlum to show them how it was done. During a raid, Odlum refused to wear a helmet, so that his men could recognize him at all times. By the time he arrived at Vimy, Odlum was a brigadier-general. His skill and luck with the trench raid, however, did not prevent the disastrous attack of March 1, 1917.

"I am not sacrificing
one man unnecessarily."
— Arthur Currie,
after cancelling a trench raid

raid was coming. They put on gas masks, carefully positioned their machine guns, and mowed down the Canadians as they approached. The wind changed and blew the poison gas back in the attackers' faces. And it ate into the lungs of the wounded lying in no man's land. Of the 1,700 men who took part in the raid, only 685 returned.

(Opposite) War artist Howard Mowat depicts men leaving on a night raid and (right) engaging in grim combat in an enemy trench. A key weapon in these raids was the small hand grenade known as the Mills bomb (left, at actual size). The bomb thrower removed the pin, kept the lever down with his hand and lobbed the grenade into a dugout or trench. (Top) Two days after the March 1st raid a truce was declared. German soldiers carried the dead and wounded from the raid and handed them over to the Canadians.

DOING THE VIMY GLIDE

After the March 1st raid, training for the main attack on Vimy was stepped up. Arthur Currie knew he couldn't afford any more setbacks. Behind the lines, a scaled replica of the German trench system was laid out with white tape. Signposts labelled the enemy trenches and coloured flags marked every stronghold and machine gun — and even tangles of barbed wire. The men practised on it every day.

And they practised with stopwatches. Split-second timing was essential as the advance would take place under a "creeping barrage." It would begin with the big guns of the artillery firing together. The men would advance and wait for the firing to stop. The guns would then aim for their next target and another group of men would advance once again. If they moved too quickly, they would be killed by their own guns. If they moved too slowly, the enemy would recover and begin firing at them. As Julian Byng told them, "Chaps, you shall go over exactly like a railroad train, on the exact time, or you shall be annihilated."

Instruction sessions (opposite, top left) and rehearsals on a scaled replica of the German trench system (opposite, top right) occurred daily in the weeks before the Vimy attack. While the infantry rehearsed advancing under a "creeping barrage" (below), pack horses carried shells up to the front (opposite, bottom) for the artillery. (Right) This iron stake for barbed wire could be quietly screwed into the ground. (Far right) German soldiers practise cutting barbed wire.

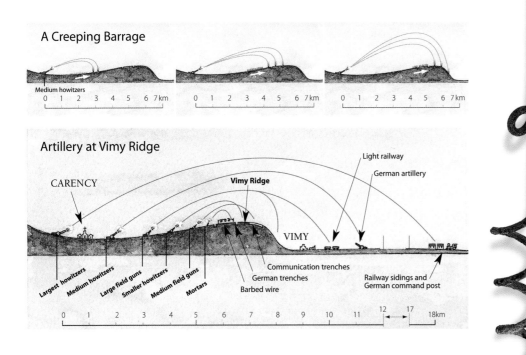

A Creeping Barrage

Medium howitzers
0 1 2 3 4 5 6 7 km

0 1 2 3 4 5 6 7 km

0 1 2 3 4 5 6 7 km

Artillery at Vimy Ridge

Light railway

German artillery

CARENCY

Vimy Ridge

VIMY

Largest howitzers · Medium howitzers · Large field guns · Smaller howitzers · Medium field guns · Mortars

Communication trenches
German trenches
Barbed wire

Railway sidings and German command post

0 1 2 3 4 5 6 7 8 9 10 11 12 17 18km

Blowing the Barbed Wire

Huge bales of fiercely barbed steel wire (top) were used to protect enemy positions. The moans of dying men trapped on barbed wire were a haunting memory of the Somme. Julian Byng was determined to get a new invention called the No. 106 Fuse. It caused high-explosive shells to explode on contact with barbed wire, blowing huge holes in it. When the No. 106 fuses arrived at Vimy in January, Byng knew he had another key to victory.

(Below) Members of the counter-battery unit use sound-ranging to help locate enemy guns. This information would then be sent back by field telephone (bottom, left) to the artillery officers operating the big guns like this howitzer (left). On the morning of the Vimy attack, the Canadians managed to knock out 176 of the 212 German guns. Information from aerial photographs (opposite, left) was invaluable. The two parallel zig-zag lines (seen in the centre) are the opposing front-line trenches at Vimy.

THE WIZARD OF COUNTER BATTERY

Byng and Currie knew that as soon as they began their artillery barrage, the Germans would fire their big guns back. But what if they could locate the enemy guns and knock them out first? This daunting challenge was thrown to 29-year-old Andrew McNaughton. "Andy" McNaughton was an oddball — he slept on the floor and kept a lion cub as a pet. But he had a keen scientific mind that was perfect for what the army called "counter battery."

McNaughton's counter-battery unit attracted other good brains that helped develop two ingenious methods of locating guns — by flash and by sound. Both flash-spotting and sound-ranging required a series of manned posts along the front that

fed information back to McNaughton's headquarters. Before long, his team was able to determine the position of a German gun to within 22 metres, and the type and calibre of the gun in under three minutes. They also used all the information they could glean from trench raids and German prisoners, and from aerial photographs taken from observation balloons and by the daring pilots of the Royal Flying Corps.

The British army's high command looked on each of us as somebody who ought to have his head read. To them this wasn't war at all; this was some sort of fandango going on."

— Major Andrew McNaughton on his counter-battery unit

"It wasn't a very comfortable feeling."

Once, when gathering information from 1,200 metres up in an observation balloon, (above, left and right) Andy McNaughton (below) came under enemy fire. "Suddenly there was the terrific roar of a naval shell bursting close to us," he recalled, "with nothing between us and the burst except a wicker basket. It wasn't a very comfortable feeling." McNaughton used his expertise to calculate the position of the German gun and telephoned it to his staff on the ground. Allied long-range guns bombarded the German position and McNaughton was able to return to earth safely.

WAR IN THE AIR

As the men on the ground prepared for the attack, the battle for the air over Vimy was already underway. The Germans had fewer planes than the Allies. But the skill and daring of their pilots — particularly the man known as the "Red Baron," Manfred von Richthofen — more than made up for this. After seeing a dogfight in the sky, one Canadian soldier wrote, "one cannot help admiring the grace and skill with which the Red Fellow handles his machine and his audacity in painting his plane red. . . ."

The famous Canadian pilot Billy Bishop officially became an ace over Vimy on April 7, 1917. His target was a German observation balloon. Just as he was about to dive on it, he heard machine-gun fire from a German fighter plane coming right at him. Bishop fought back and shot down his attacker. But then he saw that the German balloon had been lowered to the ground. Disobeying orders, Bishop swooped down and fired on the balloon, setting it aflame. The steep dive caused his engine to fail. As he glided low over the German lines, he prepared for either death or capture. Then, suddenly, his engine kicked in and Bishop streaked for home, just above the heads of the startled enemy gunners. By the end of April, Bishop had downed seventeen planes and become the squadron's leading ace.

Manfred von Richthofen (right) downed 80 planes before he was shot down in April 1918. This crashed Sopwith Camel (far right) may have been one of the "Red Baron's" victims. Billy Bishop, Canada's greatest ace (opposite, left), had 72 kills to his record, and survived the war. The goggles (below) are of the kind he would have worn. C.R.W. Nevinson's dramatic painting (opposite) depicts Bishop in action.

**"It's no child's play to circle above German artillery batteries...
with your machine tossing about in [the] air while being tortured by exploding shells and black shrapnel puffballs coming ever nearer. . ."**

— Canadian flying ace
Billy Bishop,
describing aerial
observation at Vimy

THE WEEK OF SUFFERING

Near the end of March, the 15-inch (38-cm) howitzers were hauled into place beside the other big guns behind the lines. This was a sure sign that the attack was drawing near. Each of these monsters weighed 20 tonnes and hurled a 1,500-pound (680-kg) shell. On April 2nd, the next phase of the artillery plan was put into action. Over the next seven days, 50,000 tonnes of high explosives would be fired on the German defences. "Shells poured over our heads like water from a hose," one Canadian recalled, "and battered the area into a pockmarked wilderness of mud-filled craters."

The Germans called this "the week of suffering." Food supplies could not be brought forward, so their soldiers went hungry. And there was no chance of sleep with the constant firing and the fear that an attack would take place at any moment. By April 6th, Good Friday, senior Canadian officers knew that the attack would be on the 9th, Easter Monday. The news that day that the Americans had joined the Allies in the war boosted spirits as battle preparations continued in the trenches and tunnels.

(Opposite, top) Canadian gunners wave artillery shells for the camera. Thousands of shells like these and like this 18-pound (8.16-kg) shrapnel shell (opposite, right) were fired on German trenches from Allied guns (opposite, bottom). The constant bombardment interrupted German supply columns (above) and the delivery of food for the soldiers, and ammunition for the giant German guns (right).

ZERO HOUR APPROACHES

"What a contrast to the real object of this Holy Day," one soldier wrote in his diary on Easter Sunday, April 8, 1917. "I never heard such shelling as last night." It was a bright and beautiful spring day and in the afternoon, military bands played lively tunes as the men took their positions for the attack. As thousands of men waded through mud-filled trenches or headed down into the subways, they called out to each other, "There go the Van Doos!" or "Good luck, Toronto!"

There was no sleep that night as the men stood in full battle gear in the dank subways or the freezing jump-off trenches. Some of them scribbled "just in case" letters home. As midnight passed and the minutes ticked away, Arthur Currie asked the officers to check and re-check their watches. (He had already sent out a patrol to make sure all the barbed wire had been cut.) Rain mixed with sleet began falling. Later it turned into a near-blizzard of snow. Before dawn the front was suddenly quiet. At two minutes before Zero Hour the order was whispered along the trenches, "Fix bayonets." The seconds ticked by till 5:30 a.m. — and then the whole world exploded.

(Above, left) Behind the lines, a soldier reads his mail. On April 8 some of the men had received Easter postcards (right), and many of them had written letters home like the one quoted opposite.

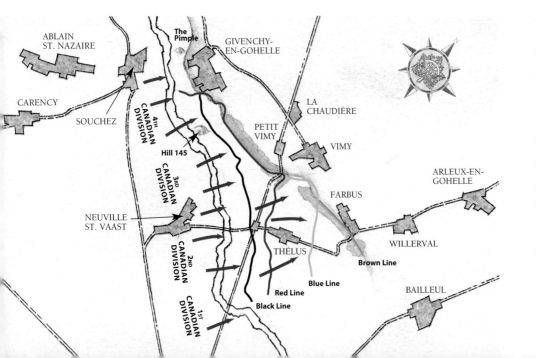

The Plan Each carefully timed stage of the attack was marked on a map with coloured lines. The "creeping barrage" would begin at dawn and the first troops would reach the Black Line in 35 minutes. On the left side, the 3rd and 4th Divisions, who had less ground to cover, were expected to be over the top of the ridge to the Red Line in 20 minutes. On the right side, the 1st and 2nd Divisions had farther to go, and for them there were four target lines — Black, Red, Blue and Brown. The Brown Line was on the eastern side of the ridge and they were expected to reach it by 1:18 in the afternoon. The heavily defended Pimple was not scheduled to be taken till the following day.

If this must be goodbye . . . "I hope not, but this may be a note of farewell, for we attack tomorrow morning. If this must be goodbye I must try to acknowledge the unrepayable debts I owe you for love and tenderness, encouragement and sympathy, and high ideals all through my life — you have been the best of mothers to us — and to ask forgiveness — I know it has been granted already — for the pain and trouble I have sometimes cost you. God bless you for all your goodness! . . . I feel very cheery, and if my feelings are an index I should get through this alive, but one never knows. I trust humbly in God, whichever way the issue goes and ask success for our arms, forgiveness for our sins and rest after much toiling."

— Lieutenant William George McIntyre, 29th (Vancouver) Battalion,
writing to his mother on April 8, 1917. He was killed the next day.

THE BATTLE BEGINS

"Imagine the loudest clap of thunder you ever heard, multiplied by two and prolonged indefinitely," is how one soldier described the battle's opening salvo. Thousands of shells rained down on the German trenches — and on German gun emplacements, just as Andy McNaughton had planned. Then it was the infantry's turn. "As soon as the artillery barrage opened up, away we went, and all you could see was smoke and Fritz [Germans] running," was an infantryman's description.

(Below) It was the greatest artillery barrage in the history of warfare. The far-off booming of the guns could even be heard in England.

Arthur Currie's 1st Division had the farthest to go — 5 kilometres to Farbus Wood on the far side of Vimy Ridge. The infantrymen overcame the first German trench line in half an hour, but faced murderous machine-gun fire as they approached the Red Line. Despite heavy casualties, the men of the 1st Division pushed on. By 1:30 p.m. they had reached the Brown Line on the other side of the ridge and seized the German guns in Farbus Wood. The 2nd and 3rd Divisons had reached their targets by that time as well.

The unheard-of had happened! A battle had gone according to plan and three-quarters of Vimy Ridge was in Canadian hands by lunchtime. But at the ridge's highest point something was very wrong. What had happened to the 4th Division?

(Above) Only a few tanks — a recent invention — were used at Vimy. They were soon knocked out by artillery. (Below) Battalions signalled with special flags to circling aircraft that they had reached their target positions.

For Valour As the 1st Division advanced on the Red Line, Private William Milne (left) from Moose Jaw, Saskatchewan, saw corpses piling up before a German machine gun (below, right). He jumped into a nearby shell hole, crawled forward through the mud, and threw a Mills bomb that destroyed the gun. Just over an hour later he saw bullets coming from a haystack right in front of him. His steady arm threw another Mills bomb that destroyed the gun hidden in the haystack. He then charged on the German gun crew, who surrendered to him. Milne was awarded the Victoria Cross (above) for his bravery, but the medal was given to his family — Milne was killed later that same day.

Hill 145

The 4th Division had been given the toughest job of all — taking Hill 145, the highest point on the ridge, and the most strongly defended. But the 4th Division had lost many men and experienced officers in the March 1st trench raid, and one of their surviving officers had made a fateful decision. He had asked the artillery to leave one German trench undestroyed so that his men could use it for cover from the guns on the hill above. Instead, they found it full of Germans firing furiously at them! In the first six minutes of the attack, one-half of the men of the 87th Battalion, the Grenadier Guards of Montreal, were cut down.

By the afternoon, the advance of the 4th Division was in chaos. The Germans were still able to fire down at the Canadians from Hill 145, and from the Pimple as well. Once night fell, they could move in reinforcements. The Canadians *had* to take Hill 145 before dark. But how could they find the men to do it? In desperation, the commanders called in the

85th Battalion of Nova Scotia. The 85th had only been in France for a month, working as a labour unit. Its men knew how to dig trenches and haul supplies. But could they fight?

By 5:45 p.m. the men of the 85th were crouched below Hill 145, waiting for an artillery barrage to knock out enemy guns. But the barrage never came. So at 6:45 p.m. they charged anyway — directly into fierce machine-gun fire. As some men fell, the others kept advancing, firing with rifles and Lewis guns. When the Germans manning the five machine guns saw the swarm of attackers, they fled — with the Nova Scotians howling after them. In one hour of bloody fighting, the men of the 85th had captured Hill 145. The work battalion had done the impossible.

They did magnificently . . . "Dear Father and Mother: Yes, we were in it up to our eyes. And if I was proud of the battalion before, I'm a thousand times more so now. They did magnificently. At the last minute we were given a tough nut to crack. Some splendid chaps went down but they were an incentive to our chaps to see they did not die in vain. Our name is written down all right, now."

— Major J.L. Ralston, 85th Battalion, Nova Scotia Highlanders

(Left) The fight to overtake the enemy positions below Hill 145 on April 10th was short but brutal. The 50th (Calgary) Battalion lost 228 men. (Right) The ruins of Farbus village. (Opposite, middle) Thirty-five Japanese-Canadians died during the assault on the Pimple. (Opposite, right) The task of burying the dead begins.

"He was so badly torn . . ."

"Harry Waller was blasted into the mouth of the [old mine] shaft. He was so badly torn that we had an awful time getting him out. . . . He was in great pain, his back twisted all out of shape. His left arm and right leg were broken . . . pieces of shrapnel stuck out of his head. His eyes filmed over and shut out the past — and present. . . . Art Waller knelt over the prostrate body of his brother, Harry, and wept bitterly. . . . "

— Victor Wheeler, describing the death of his best friend during the battle for the Pimple. Harry Waller was 22 years old — one of three Waller brothers in the 50th (Calgary) Battalion.

KING OF THE PIMPLE

"How did the Germans let us do it?" wondered Captain H.S. Cooper of the Princess Pats as he stood on the crest of Vimy Ridge on the evening of April 9th. But the battle was not yet over. The enemy still controlled the woods below Hill 145. The next morning, a battalion from Calgary and another from Winnipeg forced the Germans to retreat after an hour of bloody combat. That left the Pimple, a wooded knoll bristling with German machine guns, at the northern tip of the ridge. Before dawn on April 12th, three battalions from Western Canada groped up the hill in a raging snowstorm. In the blinding snow and darkness, the German machine gunners were unable to see the attackers. After a fierce hand-to-hand struggle, the Pimple fell to the soldiers from Western Canada — though half of them were killed or wounded. Their commanding officer reported on the victory to headquarters with the claim, "I am King of the Pimple."

Vimy Ridge — the most powerful German bastion on the Western Front — was now completely in Allied hands.

"From the crest the whole plain of Douai lay out at our feet. The vista was one of peaceful-looking villages nestling in green woods . . . " — Private William Kentner

"**Every American will feel a thrill of admiration and a touch of honest envy at the achievement of the Canadian troops. . . . No praise of the Canadian achievement can be excessive.**"

— *New York Tribune*

> **"The Canadian has lived down his reputation as a 'rag-tag' army and is now considered the best in the B.E.F. . . . One feels proud to be a Canadian out here now."** — Captain Claude Williams, writing home after Vimy

AFTERMATH

Vimy Ridge was the deepest advance the Allies had made in over two years of war. The Canadians had shown how a carefully planned and well-executed assault could lead to victory. And the world took notice. In his diary, Prime Minister Robert Borden jotted down, "all newspapers ringing with praise of Canadians." Prince Rupprecht of Bavaria, who had commanded the Germans at Vimy, wrote to his father, "I doubt that we can recapture the Vimy Ridge. This leads to the question, 'Is there any sense in continuing the war?'" But the victory at Vimy did not bring about an end to the war. The British and French were unable to follow up on the Canadians' success. The Germans retreated and dug in new trenches, and the stalemate continued. Vimy Ridge, however, would remain in Allied hands for the rest of the war.

After Vimy, Julian Byng was promoted and Arthur Currie became the commander of the Canadian Corps — now considered the élite troops of the British Army. Currie protested when he was ordered to take his men back to Ypres in October of 1917. He said it would cost the lives of 16,000 men to finish off a disastrous British attack near a village called Passchendaele. Fighting in a sea of mud, shell craters and gas, the Canadians pushed back the enemy at Passchendaele. But 15,064 of them were left dead or wounded, just as Currie had predicted. At home, the ever-increasing number of telegrams announcing the death of a husband, son or brother made Canadians question the terrible cost of the war.

(Opposite) Canadian soldiers returning after the battle of Vimy Ridge. They had made greater advances and captured more guns and prisoners than any Allied offensive since the start of the war. (Right) King George V (at left) visited Vimy after the battle and knighted Arthur Currie (in centre). (Far right) Prime Minister Robert Borden and Sir Arthur Currie review the troops as the war continues.

ARMISTICE

A breakthrough in the Western Front did not come until the spring of 1918. But it was the Germans who made it — smashing through the British lines south of Arras on March 21st. A week later and a world away, a riot exploded in Quebec City when police tried to arrest men for refusing to serve in the army. To provide more troops for the war, Robert Borden's government had passed a conscription law that required all able-bodied men to enlist. Many Canadians, particularly French-Canadians, were bitterly opposed to this law. Four people were killed before the rioting ended.

The Germans' spring offensive of 1918 proved to be their undoing. Their advances soon bogged down and by summer the Allies counter-attacked. The Canadians spearheaded a successful assault at Amiens on August 8th — a day the German commander Ludendorff called "the blackest day of the war." But even in retreat the Germans fought on, and it was not until November 11th, the day we now mark as

"The war will not last forever; but the memory of it, the suffering of it, the incalculable waste of it, will last f

Remembrance Day, that an armistice was signed. Canadians at home poured into the streets to celebrate. For the soldiers at the front there was relief, mixed with exhaustion — but little joy. As one of them wrote, "It was quite some time before the news filtered through our benumbed minds that the war was over and that we'd survived."

◄ that remains of our lives."

— Lieutenant Coningsby Dawson

(Opposite, left) As they push into Belgium, Canadians celebrate in a liberated town. They entered the town of Mons (opposite, right) on November 10, 1918, and the armistice was signed at 11:00 the next morning. (Below, left) A plaque near Mons commemorates 25-year-old George Price, who was killed by a sniper's bullet two minutes before the ceasefire. (Below) A painting by Ernest Sampson depicts the Armistice Day celebrations in Toronto.

**"I have always felt that Canadian nationality was born at the top of Vimy Ridge. . . .
There was a feeling that we had mastered the job and that we were the finest troops on earth.
This is where Canadian nationality first came together. . . . "** — E.S. Russenholt, 44th (Manitoba) Battalion

THE LEGACY
The men of the Canadian Expeditionary Force came home to a war-weary country. Canada had lost 60,661 of its youngest and finest citizens in the most brutal war the world had ever seen. Names like Ypres, the Somme and Passchendaele made people shudder. But not Vimy. That name was one that every schoolchild learned, a name carved on the Peace Tower in Ottawa. Vimy stood for Canada's emergence as a nation from under Britain's shadow. Vimy was a symbol of Canadian ingenuity, skill and daring. Canada's participation in the war won it a place at the table at the Paris peace talks in 1919, and a vote in the League of Nations, a forerunner to today's United Nations. And in 1931, the Statute of Westminster gave Canada control of its own foreign policy.

Today, some people question "the Vimy myth." Should Canadians take pride, they ask, in a battle that cost 10,602 casualties and 3,598 deaths? A battle that made little difference to the outcome of the war? The Great War itself (as it was once called) is now seen as having led to World War II, an even more murderous conflict that engulfed the world only twenty years later.

Yet, in remembering the stories of those young men who faced death on that long-ago Easter Monday, what Canadian is not moved by their bravery and sacrifice?

(Opposite) Soldiers wave as a troopship arrives in Canada. The first soldiers started returning in March of 1919. It took five months before all 300,000 men of the Canadian Expeditionary Force were home. Celebrations for returning battalions (left) were held in towns and cities across the country. Over 700,000 Canadians out of a population of 8 million had served in the war. (Right) Today, mementoes like this helmet and kit bag are treasured by many Canadian families.

"I dreamed I was in a great battlefield. I saw our men . . . being mowed down by the sickles of death. . . . Suddenly . . . I saw thousands marching to the aid of our armies. They rose in masses . . . and entered the fight to aid the living. . . . They were the dead. Without the dead we were helpless. So I have tried to show in this monument to Canada's fallen, what we owed them and we will forever owe them."

— Walter Allward, sculptor and designer of the Vimy Memorial

THE MEMORIAL

Sculptor Walter Allward's dream of dead men arising from the earth inspired his design for Canada's memorial to its war dead in France. It didn't take long for Hill 145 on Vimy Ridge to be selected as the most fitting location. Eighty-five hectares around the hill were granted to Canada by France in 1922. Work began there three years later, but it was a difficult job. The site was filled with tunnels, craters and unexploded shells and grenades. Many men were injured by explosions as they cleared the area with picks and shovels. More than 15,000 tonnes of concrete were required for the base of the monument. On top of it rose two white marble pylons, each 69 metres high, representing Canada and France united in war and peace. Twenty marble statues, each with symbolic meaning, were carved. The largest depicts a weeping woman and represents a young nation mourning her fallen sons.

A painting of the Vimy Memorial by William Longstaff (above) depicts sculptor Walter Allward's dream of dead soldiers arising from their graves. (Right) Stonecarvers work on The Breaking of the Sword, one of the two groups of figures placed on the rampart facing the Douai Plain (opposite, top left). Between them stands the largest sculpture, a weeping woman representing the Spirit of Canada (opposite, top left and right), who looks down on the symbolic tomb of a fallen soldier. (Far right) Veterans and their families surround the monument after its unveiling on July 26, 1936. (Opposite, bottom) Statues of Justice and Peace crown the highest points of the pylons, and, at their base (opposite, top, centre) the Spirit of Sacrifice throws the torch to his comrades.

On July 26, 1936, 100,000 people gathered on Vimy Ridge for the unveiling ceremony. Five ocean liners had brought 6,200 pilgrims from Canada — among them many veterans and war widows. After King Edward VIII unsheathed the statue representing the spirit of Canada, crowds swarmed the monument. They looked at the seemingly endless list of names carved on it — for the 11,000 soldiers whose bodies had never been found. In cemeteries nearby stood rows of white gravestones, each carved with a maple leaf. Today, these carefully tended graves still pay tribute to the thousands of husbands, sons and brothers who never came home from Vimy Ridge.

The Victoria Cross at Vimy

It is a plain, bronze medal — but the Victoria Cross is the highest award for gallantry in the British Commonwealth. Four Canadian soldiers at Vimy won the VC, but only one of them survived the war.

The youngest medal-winner was 24-year-old Private **William "Willie" Milne** (see p. 33). At 41, Private **John G. Pattison** was the oldest, and even had a son serving with him in the 50th (Calgary) Battalion. During the attack in the woods below Hill 145 on April 10, 1917, fire from a German machine-gun nest was cutting down Pattison's company. Dodging bullets, Pattison jumped from one shell hole to another and then lobbed three Mills bombs, disabling the gun. He then rushed forward and held the position with his bayonet until others could join him. He was killed in action two months later. During his burial at Vimy, his son wore his medal.

Sergeant **Ellis Sifton**, 25, from Wallacetown, Ontario, never knew he'd won the VC. He, too, disabled an enemy machine gun — by charging directly at it and clubbing and bayoneting its crew. As he supervised the taking of prisoners, a wounded German shot him. Sifton is buried near Vimy in a cemetery built in a shell crater.

Two German machine guns stood in the way of Major **Thain MacDowell**, 26, early on the morning of April 9th. He bombed them both and then chased one of the gunners down the steps of a deep tunnel. As he rounded a corner in the tunnel, MacDowell came face to face with 77 enemy soldiers. Thinking quickly, MacDowell looked over his shoulder and shouted orders back — as if he had many men behind him. The bluff worked and the Germans raised their hands in surrender. But how could he take all these prisoners without being discovered and overwhelmed? MacDowell divided the Germans into groups and sent them up the stairs a dozen at a time. There, two of Macdowell's men managed to hold the prisoners until help came.

After the war, Thain MacDowell had a successful career and lived until 1960. **Billy Bishop** (see p. 26) died only four years before him. He, too, received the Victoria Cross, for single-handedly attacking a German airfield on June 2, 1917.

Vimy Veterans

At the end of the war, **Sir Arthur Currie** was hailed by the British prime minister as one of the best commanders in the British forces. In 1920 he became principal and vice-chancellor of McGill University, and held that position until his death in 1933. **Julian Byng** became Viscount Byng of Vimy and served as Canada's governor general from 1921–1926. His term is best remembered for his refusal to dissolve Parliament at Prime Minister Mackenzie King's request, which became known as the King-Byng Affair. The Lady Byng trophy for gentlemanly conduct in hockey was donated by his wife in 1925. Another Vimy veteran, Major **Georges Vanier** of the Van Doos, became Canada's first French-Canadian governor general in 1959. **Andrew McNaughton** (see p. 25) became a senior commander of the Canadian forces in Europe in World War II. But he feuded with the minister of defence, **J.L. Ralston**, who was also at Vimy (see p. 35), and resigned in 1943. **Victor Odlum** (see p. 20) also served in World War II, as a major-general, and later became Canada's first ambassador to China. **Will R. Bird** (see p. 18) was haunted by his wartime experiences and wrote about them in several books. He lost his only son in World War II. **Gregory Clark** (see p. 9) also became a writer and journalist.

Just think what those who never came home might have accomplished.

Glossary

ace: a combat pilot who has brought down at least 5 airplanes.

Allies: the nations that fought against Germany, Austro-Hungary and the Ottoman Empire in World War I. They were France, Great Britain and its empire, Italy, Russia, Romania, Serbia and, after April 1917, the U.S.A.

army units: the British forces during World War I were organized as follows: an **Army** had 2 or more **Corps**; a **Corps** contained several **Divisions**; a **Division** had 3 **Brigades**; a **Brigade** had 4 **Battalions**; a **Battalion** contained 4 **Companies**, and each **Company** had 4 **Platoons** made up of 12 men. The Canadian **Corps** at Vimy had 4 **Divisions**.

armistice: a truce, or stopping of hostilities, by agreement of both sides.

artillery: weapons such as big guns and cannons, and the forces that use them.

B.E.F: British Expeditionary Force, a name for the British troops on the Western Front.

bayonet: a sharp, steel blade attached to the end of a rifle.

casualties: a term for the dead and wounded from a battle.

chlorine gas: a poison gas that smelled just like swimming-pool chlorine. Mustard gas had a mustard-like odour and a brownish-yellow colour.

conscription: a government policy that requires people to serve in the army.

creeping barrage: an infantry advance behind a line of artillery fire.

dominion: a self-governing country within the British Empire. Canada, Australia, New Zealand and South Africa were all dominions during World War I. Newfoundland was a British colony.

dugout: a space dug underground or in the wall of a trench, often used as an officer's quarters, a gun emplacement or a storage room.

fandango: a lively Spanish dance.

Fritz: an Allied nickname for a German soldier.

geophone: a listening instrument that looks like a doctor's stethoscope. It was used by tunnellers (called "sappers") to listen for enemy sappers.

grenade: a small bomb that can be thrown by hand.

"going West": a slang expression for dying.

howitzer: a short gun that can fire high in the air.

infantry: soldiers trained to fight on foot.

League of Nations: an international organization formed in 1920 to try to prevent another world war.

Lewis gun: a small, portable machine gun. Billy Bishop holds one in his plane on p. 27.

militia: a volunteer military force that is called on in times of emergency.

mortar: a short large-bore cannon that can fire shells at a high angle.

puttees: strips of cloth that were wrapped around a soldier's ankles and shins.

Princess Pats: a nickname for soldiers of the Princess Patricia's Light Infantry Regiment of Canada.

re-enactor: a person interested in military history who wears authentic uniforms and re-enacts battles.

shrapnel: metal from exploded shells and pieces of small shot, usually lead, that were contained within exploding shells.

Stonehenge: a prehistoric monument in England made up of huge standing stones.

Van Doos: a nickname in English for the Royal 22nd (Vingt-Deuxième) Regiment of Quebec.

Index

Page numbers in italics refer to illustrations or maps

Selected Bibliography

Berton, Pierre. *Marching as to War*. Toronto: Random House of Canada, 2001
        — *Vimy*: Toronto: Random House of Canada, 1986

Bird, Will R. *Ghosts Have Warm Hands*. Nepean: CEF Books, 1968

Bishop, Arthur. *Our Bravest and Our Best*. Toronto: McGraw-Hill, Ryerson, 1995

Christie, Norm. *For King & Empire*. Nepean: CEF Books, 1996
        — *Winning the Ridge*. Nepean: CEF Books, 1998
        — *Letters of Agar Adamson*. Nepean: CEF Books, 1997

Freeman, Bill, and Richard Nielsen: *Far from Home*. Toronto: McGraw-Hill Ryerson Ltd., 1999
    (Also a documentary film series available from the National Film Board.)

Goodspeed, D.J. *The Road Past Vimy*. Toronto: Macmillan, 1969

Granatstein, J.L. *Hell's Corner*. Vancouver: Douglas & McIntyre, 2004

Granfield, Linda. *In Flanders Fields*. Toronto: Fitzhenry & Whiteside, 1995
        — *Where Poppies Grow*. Toronto: Fitzhenry & Whiteside, 2001

Greenhous, Brereton. *Canada and the Battle of Vimy Ridge*. Ottawa: Canada
    Communications Group, 1997

Macksey, Kenneth. *The Shadow of Vimy Ridge*. Toronto: Ryerson Press, 1965
        — *Vimy Ridge*. New York, Ballantine Books, 1972

Marteinson, John. *We Stand On Guard*. Montreal: Ovale Publications, 1992

Morton, Desmond, and J.L. Granatstein: *Marching to Armageddon*. Toronto: Lester &
    Orpen Dennys, 1989
        — *A Military History of Canada*. Toronto: McClelland & Stewart, 1992

Oliver, Dean, and Laura Brandon. *Canvas of War*. Vancouver: Douglas & McIntyre, 2000

Palmer, Svetlana and Sarah Wallis. *Intimate Voices from the First World War*. New York:
    William Morrow, 2003

Read, Daphne. *The Great War and Canadian Society, An Oral History*. Toronto: New Hogtown
    Press, 1978

Wood, Herbert Fairlie. *Vimy!* Toronto: Macmillan, 1967

Websites: **The Canadian War Museum**, **Library and Archives Canada**, **Veterans Affairs
Canada**, **The Canadian Legion Magazine** and **The Dominon Institute** all have websites
with useful information about World War I.

Picture Credits

Maps and diagrams are by
Jack McMaster.
Colour photographs are by Ian Brewster
unless otherwise indicated.

CWM – Canadian War Museum
LAC – Library and Archives Canada
CTA – City of Toronto Archives

Images not credited below are from
private collections. Every effort has been
made to clear copyright and correctly
attribute all photographs and quotations.
If any errors have occurred, we will
correct them in future editions.

Front cover: Enlist! Poster by
   C. J. Patterson, LAC/C-029568
4:   (Top) Toronto Public Library;
     (Bottom) Mary Evans Picture Library
     #10012223
5:   (Left) CTA/Fonds 1244 Item #729;
     (Right, top) CTA/Fonds 1244 #748;
     (Right, bottom) CTA/Fonds 1244
     #668; (Poster) CWM 1990029-001
6.   (Left, top) LAC/PA-07281;
     (Left, bottom) LAC/PA-202396;
     (Right, top) McCord Museum 5292;
     (Right, bottom) Royal 22e Régiment
     Museum
7:   LAC/PA-117875; (Postcard)
     The Granfield Collection
8:   (Map) Gord Sibley
9:   (Left) LAC/PA-000095;
     (Right) LAC/PA-000723

10: (Left, top) Gas Chamber at
     Seaford by Frederick Varley,
     CWM 19710261-0772;
     (Left, bottom) CWM 19700140-077;
     (Right) Passchendaele Memorial
     Museum
11: (Left, top) LAC/C-080027;
     (Left, bottom) CWM 19820103-011
12: LAC/PA-000914
14: LAC/PA-001148
17: (Top, left) CWM 19680113-001;
     (Top, right) LAC/PA-001370
18: Will Bird photo from Ghosts
     Have Warm Hands
20: (Left) A Night Raid by H. J. Mowat,
     CWM 19710261-0431;
     (Right) LAC/PA-202398
21: (Right) Trench Fight by
     H. J. Mowat, CWM 19710261-0434
22: (Bottom) LAC/PA-001229;
     (Top, right) LAC /PA-003666
23: (Right, bottom) The Granfield
     Collection
24: (Left, bottom) Passchendaele
     Memorial Museum;
     (Right) LAC/PA-005460
25: (Left) LAC/PA-002366;
     (Bottom) LAC/PA-034150
26: (Left) Passchendaele Memorial
     Museum; (Centre) LAC/C- 027737;
     (Right) LAC/PA-003894
27: (Left) LAC/PA-122515; (Right) War in
     the Air, 1918 by C.R.W. Nevinson,
     CWM 19710261-0517
28: (Bottom) LAC/PA-001500
29: (Bottom) The Granfield Collection
30: (Postcard) The Granfield Collection
31: Over the Top, Neuville-Vitasse,1918 by
     Alfred Bastien, CWM 19710261-0056

32: LAC/PA-001879
33: (Left, bottom) Illustration
     by Sharif Tarabay;
     (Right, top) LAC/PA- 004388;
     (Right, Middle) LAC/PA-001096;
     (Right, Bottom) Imperial War
     Museum Q23709
34–35: LAC/PA-001020
36: (Left) Capture of a German Trench
     at Vimy by W. B. Wollen, Royal
     Canadian Military Institute;
     (Right) LAC/PA-001071
37: (Top, right) LAC/PA-004352;
     (Bottom) LAC/PA-001446
38: LAC/PA-001332
39: (Left) LAC /PA-001502;
     (Right) LAC/PA–002746
40: (Left) LAC/PA-003068;
     (Right) CWM/AN19930065-429
41: (Left) Gareth Turner;
     (Right) Armistice Day, Toronto
     by Ernest Sampson, CWM
     19710261-0655
42: LAC/PA-022995
43: (Left) Glenbow Archives
     NB-16-609
44: (Left, top) Vimy Ridge by William
     Longstaff, CWM 19890275-051;
     (Bottom, left) CWM 19770315-018;
     (Bottom, right) LAC/PA-183544
45: Photos by Harry Palmer: (Top left)
     LAC-PA57/88-04-10/10;
     (Top, middle) LAC-PA57/89-05-22/03
     (Top, right) LAC-57/88-04-10/15
     (Bottom) LAC-57/88-04-20/17
Back cover: The Taking of Vimy Ridge
     by Richard Jack, CWM 8178

About the Author

Hugh Brewster is the award-winning author of many books on historical subjects, including *Anastasia's Album*, *Inside the Titanic* and the forthcoming *Dieppe*. He won the Children's Literature Roundtables of Canada Information Book Award in 2006 for *On Juno Beach* and the Honour Book for *At Vimy Ridge* in 2007. *At Vimy Ridge* is a nominee for the 2009 Norma Fleck Award and the Red Maple Award.

Acknowledgements

Thanks to Gord Sibley for his excellent design; Desmond Morton for reviewing and advising on final layouts; Linda Granfield for her support, expertise and images; Ian Brewster for photography at Vimy; Tom Deacon for his great-uncle's photos and letters; Nan Jemmett, Sue and Gerard McNally, Linda and Paul Kidney and Donald Sibley for sharing family photographs and artifacts. I'm grateful to re-enactors Nigel Bristow and Chris Barker for artifacts and advice. Nigel's uncle, Leonard Bristow, was killed in 1914. Thanks to Captain Gareth Carter; Charlotte Cardoen-Descamps at Varlet Farm; Franky Bostyn and Kristof Blieck at the Passchendaele Memorial Museum; Tim Cook and Maggie Arbour-Doucette at the Canadian War Museum; Isabelle Fernandes and Daniel Potvin at Library and Archives Canada; Chuck Loewen, David Craig and Larry Muller for reference books; Signe Ball of *In the Hills* magazine; Nancy Pearson and Sandra Bogart Johnston at Scholastic Canada Ltd.; Gregory Loughton at the RCMI; all the staff at the Vimy Memorial.

Produced by Whitfield Editions
Designed by Gordon Sibley

**Library and Archives Canada
Cataloging in Publication**

Brewster, Hugh
At Vimy Ridge : Canada's greatest World
War I victory / Hugh Brewster.

ISBN 0-439-93834-1 (bound)
ISBN 0-439-94982-3 (pbk.)

1. Vimy Ridge, Battle of, France, 1917—
   Juvenile literature. I. Title.
   D545.V5B74 2006
   j940.4'31
   C2006-902542-8

ISBN-13 0-439-94982-8

SCHOLASTIC CANADA LTD.
604 King Street West,
Toronto, Ontario, Canada
M5V 1E1

6 5 4 3 2   Printed in Canada   08 09 10 11 12